American Dreams

Reveries and Revisitations

Norman, Oklahoma
2013

FIRST EDITION, 2013

American Dreams: Reveries and Revisitations © 2013
by Norbert Krapf

ISBN 978-0-9851337-4-0

Except for fair use in reviews and/or scholarly considerations, no part of this book may be reproduced, performed, recorded, or otherwise transmitted without the written consent of the author and the permission of the publisher.

Cover Image,
Image for Section I: American Dreams, and author photo:
© Andreas Riedel 2004

MONGREL EMPIRE PRESS
NORMAN, OK

ONLINE CATALOGUE: WWW.MONGRELEMPIRE.ORG

This publisher is a proud member of

COUNCIL OF LITERARY MAGAZINES & PRESSES
www.clmp.org

Book Design: Mongrel Empire Press using iWork Pages

American Dreams

Reveries and Revisitations

by

Norbert Krapf

What thou lov'st well remains,

                                        the rest is dross.

What thou lov'st well shall not be reft from thee

What thou lov'st well is thy true heritage

                                              –Ezra Pound
                                              Canto LXXXI

So we beat on, boats against the current,

borne back ceaselessly into the past.

                                        –F. Scott Fitzgerald
                                          The Great Gatsby

To make a prairie it takes a clover and one bee,

One clover, and a bee,

And revery.

The revery alone will do,

If bees are few.

                                             –Emily Dickinson

Acknowledgments

"An American Dream" and "In the Back Seat of a Fast-Moving Car" were originally published in *Poetry Now*. "Meeting Mari Evans at Marsh" appeared in *Punchnell's*.

"Setauket, Stony Brook, Port Jefferson" appeared in the author's *Arriving on Paumanok* (Street Press, 1979); the cycles "On a Hill Near the Rhine" and "The Sunday Before Thanksgiving" in *The Sunday Before Thanksgiving* (Raincrow Press, 1999); "Walking with Walt Whitman and William Cullen Bryant" in *Bittersweet Along the Expressway: Poems of Long Island* (Waterline Press, 2000); and "Letter from a Star above Southern Indiana" in *Looking for God's Country*, published by Time Being Books. Reprinted by permission of Time Being Books. Copyright © 2005 Time Being Books.

Except for the last listed poem, all material in this book © 2013 Norbert Krapf.

Thanks also to Franconian photographer Andreas Riedel for permission to use his cover, section I, and author photos and to the Arts Council of Indianapolis for the Creative Renewal Fellowship 2011-12 that made it possible for the author to finish the last section of this book with the right music in his ears after trips on Highway 61 to Memphis, where the Minnesota Minstrel came to play, and extended time beyond twice on the Mississippi Blues Trail.

And thanks to Richard Fields for the photograph of the Hoosier Dylan poster.

Contents

I. American Dreams

An American Dream	1
The Houses of Roslyn, Long Island	2
Walking with Walt Whitman & William Cullen Bryant	3
Setauket, Stony Brook, Port Jefferson	4
Robert Bly Reads at Stony Brook	5
In a Pine Grove at Dusk	6
In the Back Seat of a Fast-Moving Car	7
The Would-be Taxidermist	8
Fishing for Childhood	9
The Best Game?	10
The Failure	11
Shifting Light	12
Speaking Woods	13
Meeting Mari Evans at Marsh	14
Letter from a Star above Southern Indiana	16

II. On a Hill Near the Rhine

The Western Union Man	21
To Become a Priest	22
Crossing the Rhine	23
On the Highest Hill	24
What the Telegram Says	25
Letter from a Buddy	26
No More Wars	27
What the Opa Says	28
A Panoramic View	29
The Owl Bookends	30

III. The Sunday Before Thanksgiving

The Sunday Before Thanksgiving	35
Turkey Dinner and Bingo	36
In the Promised Land	37
Born above a Saloon	38
The Story of the Wreck	39
In the Vessel of Oak	40
Benediction in Fine Rain	41
The Dark Side	42
The Village Elder	43
The "Record" Book	44

IV. Dots and the Pink Rose

Little Girl Dots	49
Daily Life on the Farm	50
The Flood of 1937	51
Sundays in St. Henry	52
A Pink Rose and the Opening of the Calumet	53
An Indianapolis Wedding	54
American Dream House	55
Dots at the Wheel Alone	56
A Nightmare in the Belly	57
Dots' Legacy	58

V. Behind the Kafka Curtain

Bohemian Wine Glasses	63
Approaching the West German Border	64
Children's Art at Customs	65
Phone Booth in a Czech Village	66
Nocturnal Tour of the Countryside	67

Biker Gang and Communist Police	68
Dancing Toward Prague	69
An Illegal Night in a Volvo Wagon	70
The Story of Franz and Max	71
Greg's Weird Story	72
A More or Less Happy Ending	73

VI. Old Language, New World

New Language	77
Missing Old Earth	78
The Sound of the Old Bells	79
Entreaty to Be Remembered	80
Those Left Behind	81
New Prayer	82
Legacy	83
Those Who Leave	84
Good Stories	85
About Here	86

VII. The Minnesota Minstrel in Manahatta

Welcome to NYC	91
Highway 61	92
Texas Hothand	93
Sometimes a Whole Band	94
Busy Being Born	95
A Mouth Harp	96
Ringmaster, Center Stage	97
Just Because I'm Seventy	98
Roots, Man, Roots	99
When I Play My Guitar	100

To the individuals whose stories
are reflected in the dream reveries
that make up this book

including but not limited to
Jerome, Clarence, Dorothy (Schmitt),
Katherine (Trahan), and Daniel Krapf
and Elizabeth Lamm-Krapf

as well as those not named
but who are part of the plot nevertheless
such as the masked and anonymous
minstrel from Minnesota

I. American Dreams

An American Dream

Sometimes when I'm sitting on the patio of this old house on Long Island, staring into the wooded hillside as rush-hour traffic swishes behind my back, I wonder if I have not dreamed the history of my family. Looking at the strip of woods slanting between the apartment complex at the top of the hill behind and Main Street in front of the house, I ask myself if my rural childhood–those days of hunting, hauling hay, and camping in the hills of southern Indiana–could not have taken place in a dream. Did my Bavarian ancestors leave their cobbled streets, cross the Atlantic Ocean on a crowded ship, and journey all the way to the southern Indiana wilderness in the middle of the nineteenth century? Was my father born in a room above a saloon operated by my great-grandfather, and did he move into the town where I was born and work for a quarter of a century in a chair factory? Could I have imagined the thick German accents of the aunts and uncles I seem to remember from my childhood? Those elderly people I fly home to visit in the familiar house in the woods, are they my parents? When I write poems and stories, do I dream these people and their history? Sitting here on a Long Island along the East Coast of America, staring into the woods, am I dreaming myself?

The Houses of Roslyn, Long Island

Like relics of a past civilization, the houses of Roslyn, Long Island stand uneasily on both sides of a street that was once an Indian trail. When horses and carriages transported people around the village, men built these wooden houses right on the street. A villager could step out his front door onto a horse. Now the owner of a house wakes up in the morning, opens the front door, and inhales carbon dioxide from cars and trucks as they streak along Main Street toward the Long Island Expressway. At night, when cars skid and crash together, red lights flash, and sirens weep, the houses of Roslyn, Long Island roll back away from the street on their rubble foundations. In the earliest hours of the morning, when the park is empty but all of a few interlopers, the houses mumble to one another about the good old days, but they have been around too long not to know that nostalgia is impractical, that they have no rights or recourse. Whenever a drunken car smashes into the front of one of them, rumors of a withdrawal blow up and down Main Street like dead leaves, but not one house is known to have disappeared overnight. During the day, the houses of Roslyn stand their ground and put up a good front. Those of us who live inside them, however, listen to the floors creak, the pipes clank, and the winds breathe through the attic and fall asleep uneasily every night.

Walking with Walt Whitman & William Cullen Bryant at Cedarmere

You're in a woods on a hillside overlooking a lake and a bay. Winds through the oaks, sun on the water. Standing on gravel at a bend in the washed-out lane, you look out over another century. Two bearded poets, one a quarter of a century older, shorter, and neater, stroll around a spring-fed lake. You can almost hear their boots squish in the marshy grass. The older one points out his prize copper beech, Japanese maples, ancient black walnut, mound of rhododendron, and watercress along the brook overflowing into the bay. He motions toward the boat house, his guest nods, and they row across clear water. As they disembark, the younger poet asks a question as he points at a gothic mill, then glances back at the lake as they climb stairs to the eighteenth century Quaker farmhouse. They sit on a bench in a formal boxwood garden and listen to water spill out of a fountain. The younger poet stands up to watch a Canada goose and her five goslings wobble past a rabbit on the lawn slanting toward the bay. When the shadows touch on the surface of the lake below, the older poet puts his hands on the shoulder of the younger, guides him onto the latticed piazza into the farmhouse.

You find yourself alone again in the woods that once belonged to the older poet. Sun on your face, wind in your beard, you read aloud to yourself these lines the younger poet wrote in his seventies:

> (For song, issuing from its birth-place, after fulfillment, wandering,
> reck'd or unreck'd, duly with love returns.)

You look up and see a full sail on the Sound and know these are now your poets, your woods, your sun, wind, and water; and this is your place.

Setauket, Stony Brook, Port Jefferson
–for Annie and Vince Clemente–

A thousand miles from where you grew up, you walk down narrow streets looking at shingle houses you might have played in as a child. Squinting at an empty rocker on a porch, you hear wood rocking across wood and see your mustachioed grandfather looking right past you. In yards where tiger lilies bloom, a June sun filters through leaves of a ship-mast locust around whose rough bark you may have circled with neighborhood children. At the museum, you walk into the shade of a barn and remember the sweet scent of hay and the warmth of animals breathing in the dark. In the next building you walk up to a painting of a happy boy holding by the hind legs a rabbit he's pulled from a wooden trap and feel the thumping in the burlap bag you grasped as you finished making the rounds before leaving for school. At the derelict mill, you roll across waves of reeds as red-winged blackbirds warble you to a pond where you dangled a cane pole over cattails. Out on a shady country lane, you hear quail whistling in a field where a cow bell jangles. Standing on the sandy point overlooking the Sound, you see the sun rippling on the water which keeps rolling to the shore in a rhythm you can't possibly know, but are sure you remember, from your childhood in the interior.

Robert Bly Reads at Stony Brook
(the 1970s)

In the lecture hall, we sit in semicircular rows at table-counters like customers awaiting short-order food. A man in a red shirt, vest, and scarf with red Norwegian hair ambles down the aisle. "The Minnesota cowboy!" I whisper in my wife's ear. When he begins to recite his poems, his hands rise above his head like delicate, long-necked white birds. They mime the rhythm of his lines, draw us out of ourselves, stir our feelings around the amphitheater like the blotches of snow gusting high above our heads in the Long Island night. A great bird comes to life, flaps one wing of sadness, another of ecstasy. It rises, then plunges into the depths of southern Indiana woods, glides through valleys, climbs higher and higher between trunks of ancient trees, bursts into sunlight. I soar along with the dead murmuring in my ears. Between the flights of his poems, he fluffs his red hair, wheedles, needles, cajoles. One minute he's a threatening father, the next a consoling mother. He unpacks a stringed instrument, tunes it, plucks chords with long white fingers, and chants Yeats and Kabir. Everyone leans forward on the table-counters, swaying on elbows. When he chants Whitman, I go blind, lose all awareness of words, ride a surf of sound. I forget where I am, come back to land, wake to applause all around, see him bowing and clapping back at us.

In a Pine Grove at Dusk

Behind the dam of the front lake and the drainage pool where catfish dart back and forth across the bottom, stirring up cloudy water between them and me, beyond the row of tulip poplars and sycamores where groundhogs have burrowed passageways beneath a mat of honeysuckle and poison ivy, I steal into the pine grove which opens upon the bank of the back lake.

Brown needles cushion each step I take toward the center, where the darkness seems clustered. Turtle heads pop up to gawk across the water as I rustle cattails along the bank. Turtle doves drop through the dusk and settle in their nests. I close my eyes and float on my back across the evening air to a time I fished here on my grandmother's farm.

For a few moments, I am as buoyant as a schoolboy released from school for the summer. When bullfrogs begin to croak, I open my eyes to a soft curtain of darkness and walk slowly from this sanctuary.

In the Back Seat of a Fast-Moving Car

I'm sitting in the back of a fast-moving car. I don't know the two people in the front seat. I look down at the floor, to the left of my feet, and see in a basket a small carcass which looks like the squirrels and rabbits I skinned as a boy. I stare, but say nothing to the driver and the other person up front. They keep talking to one another, sometimes to me, as if nothing is wrong. I keep staring at the carcass. After a while, I realize that it's not an animal carcass. It's the carcass of a human baby. Its little chopped-off arms flex like the arms of a baby when it cries, but there's no sound. Then I realize that the child is mine, that I must never let anyone see it, that I must somehow get rid of it. The people in the front seat talk, talk as the car speeds through a blurred landscape and I choke on tears that slide into my mouth.

The Would-be Taxidermist

In my youth I wanted to become a taxidermist. Ads in *Field & Stream* made the prospect of keeping beautiful animals "alive" before us attractive. But for some reason, I was never able to pull the metaphorical trigger, perhaps because I stopped being able to pull the literal one. I turned from a literal into a figurative hunter, whose aim was not to kill. I wanted those beautiful animals to live forever and realized, in time, that the way for me to make that happen, if I could learn how, was to give them expanded life in words. So now I envision the fox squirrel with the creamy yellow belly and the red undertail; the raccoon with sad eyes and black-ringed tail; the rabbit with reflecting eyes, whiskers that twitch, and back feet that thump; and the quails that sing their anapestic bob-bob white song, roost with their backsides to the inside of a circle, and explode into flight at the approach of my step. To see, hear, and remember these creatures is prerequisite to keeping them alive in combinations of words eager to undermine their mortality.

Fishing for Childhood

Going back into childhood is strange. You drop your line into the waters and never know what you'll pull up. Once a baby who died before she could breathe and claims she's your sister. A priest who breathed hot and heavy when he put his hands all over you, your brothers, and many of your friends. Him you throw back into the dark muddy waters with pleasure, hoping he'll not survive long. How odd to pull in, flopping and banging against the bank, the doctor who gave your father shock treatment. You let him expire, in great gasps of trying to suck in air where water should be. People always like to ask what's your best catch ever, the big one that never got away, the biggest of them all. The press are relentless in asking this question. Well, you say, keeping your eyes modestly on the cattails and wild weeds on the bank, the best one was the god with the long white beard, soft eyes, and belly like a granddaddy catfish. I couldn't quite grasp what he was saying in that ancient language he spoke, but it sounded like a prayer full of nostalgia for the good old days when we boys could fish all day long and every hook snagged something big and marvelous.

The Best Game?

I get so tired of being asked what was your favorite childhood game. They expect you to say Kick the Tin Can or Go Fish or Hide & Seek, but those were fairly ordinary. The one where they came and took your daddy away and gave him electric shocks to calm his nerves was certainly not my favorite. Who could enjoy the game in which they said you were going to have a baby sister, and then when she was born she also died and your mother kept crying? That one was not exactly peachy. Nor was the one in which this priest salivated after little boys and pretty much had his pick and fooled their parents with every move he made because they all believed he was The Great Man. You weren't allowed to tell your parents what he was really like and you had to pretend you liked serving mass for him and loved nothing better than swallowing the host he dropped on your tongue. Maybe the most challenging game, Guess Who's coming to Dinner, was pretending you were happiest when he came to dinner and blessed the food you all ate. Yes, maybe the best game, the one that trained you most for adulthood, was Don't Worry, Be Happy. Another one we played when our parents weren't around was The Pope Knows. After all, the Pope represents God, and so He knows everything that's going on, right? Oh yes, that was a good one to play, but I can't say it was my favorite. We had so many good ones to play you can see why the ones everyone else played didn't do the trick.

The Failure

Driven to reject all I'd accomplished before, I did my best to write nothing but vile pornography. I entertained lewd and obscene thoughts, the kind I'd always done my altar-boy best to repress, but what came out instead were angelic white prayers that rose before candles guttering on an altar onto which slanted rays of light from the heavens. There I was, embarrassed to be serving mass once again when I fervently hoped to be serving the slathering goddess of Eros. I was deflated. My career was ruined. All I had earned was another merit badge on my way to becoming an Eagle Scout. To top it off, a choir began to sing Gregorian chant to celebrate my innocence.

Shifting Light

No matter how long you walk in the woods, there is always another corner to explore and more to see and hear. The shifting light that makes its way down through layers of branches and leaves puts an ever-changing hue on everything your eyes can absorb. No matter how carefully you look, how well you listen, there is always something more to see and hear. This tree has a shape you never quite noticed, an intersection of branches that was never before apparent. That rotten stump hosts an array of bugs and grubs you never detected. In the sandy mud of the creek bed are traces of an impression someone's foot once made. Could that have been you, passing through these woods in another lifetime? And the persistent song of that little bird, where could it have been that you may have heard it before, and when?

Speaking Woods

When I enter into the woods, I know I am back home. The birds, the leaves, the moss, the mushrooms are aware of my presence and acknowledge it in ways not easy to perceive. They say nothing in any language except the silent one which voices their approval by how they grow and absorb nourishment from the soil and rain. The birds do, however, sing with just a bit more gusto than they otherwise do, to my ear. After a while, you learn to recognize not only the difference between the songs of the different kinds of sparrows and finches and blackbirds and hawks and crows, but also slight differences between members of the same species. You don't have to use any words to signal your gratitude for this reception. You learn how to let your appreciation and gratitude rise up to and through your pores and release into the dank woods air. At that point, you may see your first squirrel above. You hear a voice say, within you, Ahah! The way a fox squirrel raises its bushy red tail to catch the sunlight says more than poets have found a way to communicate by making the flow of words join together in a mystical combination of syllables. In the woods, you must understand and speak woods. If woods are where you came from and where you belong, woods are where you return to find your true tongue and let it resound in your innermost ear.

Meeting Mari Evans at Marsh

It happens to my wife, but not me. I'm jealous. She crosses the street to shop at Marsh, to get some This and That and comes back with a bag full of both and a smile. This happens altogether too often. She says, pleased with her good fortune: "I saw Mari again at Marsh." "What did you talk about?" I have to know. "Oh, this and that. She does know I'm your wife," she concedes, but I feel left out of the conversation and this private community of two, though I'm the poet. I think to myself, but am too ashamed to say out loud, "Well, Mari has a poem in a stained-glass window at the new Indy airport and so do I. Why don't she and I ever meet at Marsh? I go there often. I never get to meet Mari, but you do all the time. How's come?"

One day when we are shopping at Marsh, we split, then later I find her and Mari talking right before the low-cal grape and cranberry juice I crave. There is Mari, dressed elegantly, as ever, in black. She recognizes me. "Finally," I say, "I too get to see you at Marsh!" As if that is a privilege denied for decades. I think of her marvelous poem etched in stained glass that begins, "I will bring you a whole person." "Well," Mari says, with an ironic smile, "I was at an event the other night," as I'm thinking of another great line of hers etched in that window: "I be bringing you a whole heart." She continues, with that smile: "When I was introduced as 'the Indiana Poet Laureate,' your job, one woman made quite a sour face because she thought I had taken away your job."

The truth is, I'm no longer IPL, I declined a second term, but I don't admit it. I think instead of how much heart is in Mari's poems and presence. That makes me remember another airport poem line, "An you be bringing a whole heart / a little chipped and rusty . . . " "Oh, that woman was so unhappy," Mari continues with her unrelenting smile. "Oh," I blurt, "I wish you really were Indiana Poet Laureate! You would do a great job." I imagine her saying to me, "We be bringing . . . the music of our selves."

How can I admit that no longer serving as Indiana Poet Laureate gives me more time to spend at Marsh half-looking for Mari? I keep that secret to myself, delighted to have met and spoken with her in one of my favorite Marsh haunts, the Grape and Cranberry Aisle in downtown Indianapolis, not in California where Allen Ginsberg claimed he saw Walt Whitman in a supermarket. "We be twice as strong," I can almost hear her conclude before all those beaming bottles of juice. "You bring a whole person everywhere, to every person you meet and poem you write," I think but am a bit too shy to say to the real, not the imagined, Mari Evans in Marsh, where every bottle of juice squeezed from grapes suddenly promises to transform into deep red wine.

Letter from a Star above Southern Indiana

It was a crisp fall evening, the leaves were down, smoke was rising from neighborhood chimneys, and I was walking home across an open field from a Boy Scout meeting held at the parish school. Usually I keep my eyes on the ground, but on this clear night, as the fresh air touched my cheeks, my eyes turned upwards, then soared above our new house at the edge of the woods. What I found in that southern Indiana sky was "miracle enough to stagger sextillions of infidels," as the great earth-poet Walt Whitman once said. There, burning bright above me, were so many dead stars I could never have begun to count them, if I had wanted to.

What I want to tell you now, wherever you are, whenever you read or hear this, however it is transmitted, is that even though I could not have framed the experience in just these words, even then I knew I was being blessed. Now, a thousand miles and almost fifty years away, I can tell you this: When I made out the shape of the Little Dipper, way above our house in that little woods in southern Indiana, I felt its collapsed light heading toward me, from thousands and millions of years away. When I also located the shape of the Big Dipper, so high above, I could feel its no-longer-alive radiance pouring down toward the house my parents had built for us children.

At that point, I had not yet seen or stepped inside the brick farmhouse that my father's family had built, with the help of new neighbors, when they arrived from Germany. Framed with tulip poplar from the virgin forest, it stood on a hill just inside the next county. I had not yet discovered that my mother's and father's families once lived about twenty miles apart, in the region of Bavaria known as Lower Franconia. Yet a part of me, the one that is finding these words to beam to you, understood on some level that the family who had crossed the Atlantic on a boat were walking with me under the stars toward the house I would later find so far away for my wife and children. I could not yet name all those who came before me, but felt their presence at my side, knew they were guiding me wherever I would go. I knew I must learn to speak their language, which some of us had already left behind, but which mother and father still spoke.

All who came before were walking with me toward the new house, as the light poured down on me from millions of light years before, just as I am walking with you, wherever you are, trying to speak to you in this language I hope is still yours, in this world I hope I still share with you. If you look up, as I looked up that night in southern Indiana, when the air was so fresh and clear, you may feel the light of this letter falling down toward you. You may even think you can see me in the night sky, will understand that I once walked the earth where you now walk. May this light bless you, your house, and those who come after you.

II. On a Hill Near the Rhine

The Western Union Man

It is March, 1945. A man with bushy eyebrows and mustache is standing on the porch of a "Sears and Roebuck house" he put up for his wife and ten children. He has a German name, this man, and he and his wife, whose maiden name was German, have been listening to every news report that has crackled through their radio the past several weeks. His father, dead now for many years, came to this country from Germany; but if this man knows the name of the ancestral village, he has not mentioned it to his sons or daughters. He wears silence as comfortably as a pair of old overalls. He is standing because he sees a boy dressed in a Western Union uniform walking up the hill toward the house.

To Become a Priest

An idealistic young man from a German-Catholic village decides he wants to become a priest. He has thought long about this. When he enters the seminary at the archabbey established on a hill in the southern Indiana wilderness by the Benedictines a hundred years before, his parents are happy. Their son will become the first priest, in America, on either side of the family. A conscientious young man, he studies hard and does well. After a couple of years, however, the Benedictines advise him to take a rest. "Maybe you can come back in a couple of years," the abbot tells the young man. Almost the next day, he signs up to work with Indian children at a Benedictine mission in South Dakota. Soon the family forwards a draft notice to him at St. Cloud. "While I'm in the army," he tells a brother back in southern Indiana, before he reports for duty, "I'll show them what a good priest I would be." He boasts, "They'll have to take me back."

Crossing the Rhine

He takes his basic training in Florida, leaves for Europe, and joins the 60th Infantry of the Ninth Division, First Army. It is after the Battle of the Bulge, the war is almost over, but the fighting to control the dams along the Rhine is still severe. They cross the Rhine, which makes him think of the grandfather he never met, and reach the front. When they march into the village of St. Katherine, which is as deserted as a confessional on the night of a beerfest, he wonders if any of his relatives might live there. What would they look like, he wonders. He and his buddies bed down on the straw in a farm building that makes him feel at home. The squawking of a chicken beneath a nearby shed makes him see a rectangular chicken coop on a hill in southern Indiana. As he falls asleep, he overhears a family saying prayers in German over fried potatoes and sausage. He dreams of saying mass in one of the spired churches he looked at from the outside during the day.

On the Highest Hill

The next day is Sunday, the day of the attack. The Germans shell the village of St. Katherine, studding the farm buildings with shrapnel. The ex-seminarian, an ammunition bearer, and his buddy set up their machine gun on the highest hill in the area, just outside the village of Strödt. He looks out over the wooded valley, which seems to be flying at him in bits and pieces, toward the Rhine. The air screams; he loses focus.

What the Telegram Says

The boy keeps walking up the hill toward the house in southern Indiana. The old man with the mustache whose knees begin to wobble feels he has been standing his whole life. He calls, feebly, to his wife. He finally reaches out for the telegram. His fingers can barely tear open the envelope. He reads: "THE SECRETARY OF WAR DESIRES TO EXPRESS HIS DEEP REGRET THAT YOUR SON . . . WAS KILLED IN ACTION IN GERMANY 18 MARCH 45 CONFIRMING LETTER FOLLOWS." He sobs the cry of a man who can not bear to live much longer, and puts his arms around his wife. They sink into the swing on the porch.

Letter from a Buddy

Months later, in a reply to a series of letters from a sister, comes the official news. "He was hit by shrapnel, hit in the head and died instantly." Within two days the mailman, who has come to dread walking up the hill to the wooden house, brings a letter from a soldier with a German name. Their son's buddy, he was with him when he died and wants to give them the details he knows they must crave. "We had talked about things quite a lot," he writes, "and I understand he had studied to become a priest." One incident above all he wants the family to know about. "A few minutes before he was killed, on the way to the spot where we set up our machine gun, he knelt by a tree in prayer." The buddy with the German name adds, "He was a young man of high principle." When he returns from Germany to his hometown in Michigan, he would be glad to visit them in Indiana if they wish.

No More Wars

I park my car in St. Katherine across the street from a house on the porch of which a man and woman sit. When I explain that my uncle died here in March, 1945, thirty-four years ago, the man confirms there was heavy fighting in and around the village. He is not a native, though, and suggests that if I can come back in half an hour, I can speak with the oldest man in the village of Strödt. He shows me a scar on his arm, his "souvenir," as he calls it. He pulls up his shirt and shows me where another bullet entered his back and left through his chest. He was wounded in Stalingrad. "No more wars!" he insists. "There can be no more."

What the Opa Says

Half an hour later, I park in front of a modern house where a family works in their vegetable garden. "Oh, yes," the wife says. "The Opa was here that day." Her husband, who was wounded along the Moselle, goes to fetch the old man. When the grandfather realizes I want to know about the fighting here in March of 1945, he begins to talk so fast it is difficult to follow his German. First he and his son think my uncle must have died in the tank battle in the field on the other side of their house. "We were all evacuated and sheltered in a bunker in the mountain over there," he says, pointing to a woods. He adds that he was terrified of the SS, who bullied him and wanted to know why he wasn't fighting even though he was limping around with a cane. When I explain that my uncle was in the infantry, the two confer and agree he could have died anywhere in the area, the fighting was so heavy. From a stack of official correspondence in my satchel, I pull out a letter from the buddy and read that they set up the machine gun "on a hill." "Ah," they say together. "If he died on a hill, it had to be that one over there, by the stone quarry." I look where they are pointing and watch a truck hauling a load of rock throwing up dust along a narrow road on a big hill. "I was so glad when the Americans came," the Opa says.

A Panoramic View

Standing on the top of the hill, I have a panoramic view of the valley below and the wooded hillside opposite. No movement in the entire landscape. Beyond the hill, on the other side of the valley, flows a silent Rhine. The only sounds are the sporadic barking of a dog and the mumbling of voices in the village of Strödt. No guns thud; no shrapnel whirls. All around me, in various shades of ocher and green, flourish weeds that brush against my waist and shoulders. Here, on this obscure piece of solid earth, which an army letter referred to as a clichéd "hallowed ground," I am surrounded by weeds whose names I know neither in my own language nor the tongue of my ancestors. I look around and pick delicate pink and blue wildflowers to press in my notebook. When I close my eyes in the late afternoon quiet, I feel the touch of my grandfather's hand on mine as he led me, a two-year-old, around the chicken pen on that hill in southern Indiana. The next year, not long after his son died on this hill, his heart collapsed, and he too died.

The Owl Bookends

Standing on this obscure hill, in the German dusk, is as close as I can come to the young idealist who had to leave the seminary because of "emotional strain." We never met. The only memento I have of him, except for a pile of official army correspondence, is a pair of brooding wooden "owl" bookends he once gave to my father. They were an appropriate gift, he claimed, because my father was such a "worry wart." When I look at the photograph of my uncle in his soldier's uniform, especially from the nose up, I sometimes feel I am looking at a mirror. With those same eyes, he looked out over this scene, but he probably could not see what I see. I turn, walk to the very top of the hill, and stare down the back side at the gouged-out quarry. Along the boulder-strewn crest of the hill, I notice a cluster of wild raspberry bushes sagging with fruit. I pick a handful of ripe berries, feel the juice stain my finger tips as I lift them to my mouth, and let their sweetness break on my tongue.

III. The Sunday Before Thanksgiving

The Sunday Before Thanksgiving

It was the Sunday before Thanksgiving and the leaves were raked, the grass was cut, and the garden tilled. Bales of straw for mulching the vegetable garden and the flowerbeds were stacked in perfect rows in the utility shed. New asbestos shingles were nailed fast to the roof of the brick house. In a drawer of the desk at which he sat in a spare bedroom to keep records, papers were filed in manila folders labeled in typescript and arranged alphabetically: *Alles in Ordnung.*

Turkey Dinner and Bingo

Entering the Knights of Columbus Home for the annual turkey dinner and bingo, he paused to crack a joke with his buddy Schutz the cobbler. He hobbled up the steps on the knee he busted in a car crash in the thirties. At the top, he reached for his elbow, mumbled to my mother, "My arm . . . It's never hurt this bad," and slumped. They laid him on a table. My brother, the manager of the restaurant downstairs, tried mouth-to-mouth . . . . On a back street, a siren wailed like a baby.

In the Promised Land

Eight hundred and fifty people filed past the oak coffin in twenty-four hours. Friends from St. Henry, the village where the family eventually settled after arriving from Franconia in the 1840s, buddies from the wood factory where he made chairs for twenty-five years, farmers he sold insurance to, in German, for the next quarter of a century, associates from two decades of charity work in the St. Vincent de Paul Society, and cronies he klatsched with in retirement. Some sobbed, some grinned, several insisted, "We expect him to sit up and tell us a good one." "You have my sympathy," they all said. Some, struggling as they looked down at the subdued carpet, could pronounce it only one way: "You haff my Zim-pah-tee." Huge calloused hands squeezed our softer, paler ones. Brother-in-law Alfred Schmitt, my godfather, retired county road supervisor, cleared his throat and announced: "If he ain't in the Promised Land, I never will be!"

Born above a Saloon

Born in a room above a saloon in a house that no longer stands, in a village now almost deserted. Watched teamsters hauling freight from the now defunct railroad station at Johnsville pull in for a beer and a nickel dinner—"all you can eat!"—heaped on a plate by his Prussian grandmother. Learned to drink beer on the lap of the mustachioed man his grandmother once threw out of the saloon, because he had "den Arsch voll," but later took as her second husband. Stoked and fed the fire of his father's steam-engine sawmill, snuggled a bucket of sausage next to the fire to keep it warm till noon, and watched the screaming saw rip the timber for the new village church. Wept when he had to stop school after eight years because the nearest high school was so far away and his father decided, "We can't afford a horse." Played the fiddle Saturday nights at barn dances for a few bits and some free beers. Took impish delight in irritating his business partner, a brother, by multiplying three-digit numbers in his head quick as a blitz. Holding a gigantic pretzel to his mouth at a picnic table in the English Garden in Munich, the only trip he ever took back to the old country where his grandfather was born, he broke into a grin so big he couldn't squelch it even though he saw me raising the camera.

The Story of the Wreck

Ten feet from the coffin, I heard the story of the wreck he would not talk about, from the friend who finally appeared. After a dance in a nearby town, he offered to drive the friend's 1934 Pontiac back home. Before long, in the southern Indiana night, a pair of headlights came at them on their side of the road. He asked if he should swerve to the other side; the friend, fearing insurance complications, said No! A crash. The other car turned over, the Pontiac spun around. The other driver, pinned beneath the overturned car, cried out: "Get me out of here! Get me out of here!" He hobbled over, pulled him out, drove him to the hospital. He didn't think his own injury was bad, but the doctor, after examining him, made him stay. Operations, a faulty blood transfusion, several months on his back, visits restricted to family. The doctors gave up on him. And so the limp, the refusal to wear Bermuda shorts, the tense command from the back seat, after we were old enough to drive, to Slow Down!

In the Vessel of Oak

I would bring Kuchen, blackberry and apple and peach pies, bunches of bananas, and a jug of the reddish-blue home-made wine he loved to sip from and sigh. Beside the jug I would lay his favorite twelve-gauge double barrel, the bore cleaned, the barrel oiled, the stock polished. For walking, a pair of those shoes that always reflected light, and a cane with a fine grain. I would add a jar of pickled pigs feet and bottles of Bock beer. And a jar of the molasses he craved, even though it always made him break out in hives. For long nights, a bottle of Schnapps. These I would send, in the vessel of oak.

Benediction in Fine Rain

Who loves wood shall rest in wood. We stood on a hillside where one hundred and fifty years before, shade was as deep as night in the virgin forest. Fine rain settled on our shoulders. After the priest said a prayer, we approached, arm-in-arm, to sprinkle a farewell. The best prayer in the language rose to the surface and spilled from my lips: Blessed are the dead the rain rains upon. On the day before Thanksgiving, we gave him to the southern Indiana earth.

The Dark Side

The dark side, which frayed the nerves only electricity could fuse, he saved for his family. No one priest could possibly forgive him the adolescent sin, however venial, that haunted him. He played one priest against another. "Scrupulosity," they called it, making it sound like a vice. Flying over the Atlantic to visit us in England one Christmas brought him so close to the God he feared would not have mercy, he could hardly sleep for days. Trying to father him, I could not answer the simple questions he asked so urgently. Sometimes, toward the end, we would find him sitting alone in a room, moving his lips in silence. There was always a rosary in his pocket.

The Village Elder

On Thanksgiving Day, the day after the funeral, my brother and I sat warming our hands in front of the pot-bellied wood stove in the trailer our father had bought for a "cabin." We listened to rain beat against the new fiberglass roof he had put on the sundeck overlooking the lake. "How we used to sit here and argue!" my brother chuckled. "Do you think other people saw that side of him?" I asked. "Nah!" my brother laughed. "Remember those old guys who used to sit on the benches around the courthouse?" I nodded. "That's what he had become. One of the village elders."

The "Record" Book

In the top drawer of his desk, I found a "Record" book. Between entries about certificates of deposit, loans taken out and paid off, purchases (a television, a refrigerator, the "cabin"), and a list of haircut dates and prices, he had written an undated observation: "Kindness is the virtue of love." And next to it: "Acts of charity present the key to HEAVEN." I walked outside, beneath the bare branches of the trees he sometimes counted, and looked at the neat lawn, the tilled garden, the tight roof. As if searching for a scene from a dream, I looked up at the trees, as he taught me to do. Near the corner of the house I located the sweet gums I remembered from childhood. All their star-shaped leaves had fallen and were raked away, but the spiked round fruit still swayed against a sky as soft and blue as his eyes.

IV. Dots and the Pink Rose

Little Girl Dots

Little girl Dorothy, "Dots," has chores to do on the farm, but also loves to play. With a spoon, she digs up earth beneath the granary and pretends she is tunneling to China. She loves the sound of the baby calf's first bawl, the kitten's meow, the puppy's yap, the cardinals' flinty notes, the turtle dove's long coo. Misses the sweet sound of her daddy's mandolin in the house in the winter and the purity of his tenor as he sang "Silent Night," "Stille Nacht." Why did he go away when she was so little and never come back? She loves to walk back to the little woods beyond the pasture to see the purple trillium, the Dutchman's breeches, the May apple, and the curling petals of the dogwoods. Tenses up, though, when she has to mosey over to the still to stir the corn mash. Folks in Louisville pay good bucks for this Dubois County Dew, this White Lightning, so she stirs, glances around for the revenuers who may one day appear from nowhere, put her in handcuffs, and take her away. But not today. Today this is her woods, her US of A, her world. Dots is Queen of the Woods. Somewhere, behind the trunk of an old sugar maple, hides the dream prince who will one day find her.

Daily Life on the Farm

Born in a farmhouse west of Ireland, Indiana, the fourth of six children. Lost their father when the eldest was twelve and she was six. They locked all the doors and windows at night. No electricity till the REA (Rural Electric Administration) came in, coal oil lamps instead, one of which she and older sis Frieda carried up the steps to their cold bedroom at night. Indoor pots and outhouse for the night. Had a horse and buggy but later their mother bought, with money borrowed from a brother, a Model T. Ford. Carried water in from the well, washed and dried the dishes, carried the dirty water back outside, swept the floors with a broom, dusted, cleaned windows. Walked the cows out to the pasture and brought them back to the barn for milking. Took the horse and sled to the field to bring back watermelons. Wrote out a long list of presents they all wished to receive for Christmas but got almost none of them. Thought they were "not good enough to deserve the gifts we asked for." Walked three miles every morning to school in the village and back again in the afternoon. Liked most of her classes, especially spelling, reading, geography, and Bible stories. Liked to read Hoosier dialect poet James Whitcomb Riley in the branches of the maple tree in front of the house so big sister Frieda could not find her, tattle on her, and "get her in Dutch."

The Flood of 1937

After Dorothy graduated from high school, she moved to Louisville, where she lived with her Aunt Anna and Uncle Joe Gregory for several years. Cared for the children of two Jewish families, worked in a woolen mill, took classes to learn how to become a secretary. Found a room to rent in a solid stucco home in a good neighborhood. In January of 1937, the rains came, over nineteen inches, four times the normal amount, leaving more than sixty percent of the city under water, without power. On Black Sunday, the 24th, flood conditions were the worst ever. On January 30 at 9:36 a.m., her brother Bill sent Miss Dorothy Schmitt, at 864 Fetter Ave, Louisville, Kentucky a telegraph: ARE YOU OKAY COME HOME IF YOU CAN WIRE OR CALL WILLIAM SCHMITT. Dorothy Schmitt, twenty-three, came back home, on the crest of a flood, to the hills of southwestern Indiana for good. Worked as a secretary for The Huntingburg Lumber Company for five years. Met a short man named Clarence Krapf. Liked him and his family.

Sundays in St. Henry

A short man, Arthur, brings his girlfriend to the St. Henry family home on Sunday for the noon meal, home-made wine, and music. Ten children in the family, some already full adults, others almost there. A house on top of a hill, at the end of the cemetery, on the edge of a German Catholic village, just beyond the church their father helped build. A large vegetable garden, an orchard of fruit trees, and a grape arbor. Dorothy is at first Arthur's girlfriend, Clarence is his brother, and Rita is the baby sister who plays the organ. All ten of the children, except Edgar, the oldest who left to work in Indianapolis, sing along. Clarence, also short, brings in a tray of sweet red wine made by Benno, their father. Both Benno and Clarence play the violin and music flows with wine. Dorothy likes it here, in a warm home where ten children have grown up with a good father in the house he built before WW I. Her father, a handsome man who parted his hair in the middle and played the mandolin, died when she was only six, leaving behind six young children. The grape wine, glowing with sunlight when they lift up their glasses, goes down warmly and well, but the war that would send the brothers in uniforms to defend the world against the Germans, Italians, and Japanese had not yet started. The youngest son, Jerome, had not yet left the seminary at St. Meinrad because of "nerves" to work as a volunteer with Indian children in South Dakota, had not yet been drafted and killed by shrapnel in Germany late in the war. The nearby tombstones in the cemetery did not yet contain any of their names, except Johann, father of Benno. Johann, born in Germany, came over the water with his father Michael and the rest of their family in 1846.

A Pink Rose and the Opening of the Calumet

Dorothy and Arthur dated until they needed some time apart, when Clarence received permission from his brother to take her out. The new couple had their first date in 1941, the night the Calumet Lake Pavilion opened in Jasper, Indiana. When Clarence arrived in his Chevy to pick her up, she was wearing a pink and blue flowered satin dress. He handed her a pink rose. They spent the night dancing, with friends, on the hardwood floor suspended above lake water, until 12:30 a.m. Years later, their son, unaware that his parents had their first date the night the Calumet opened, went there on Saturday nights with friends. A band from Louisville played rockabilly, which his friends and the girls in his class loved—the guys in the band always got their first picks of which girls to take home. The oldest son of Dorothy and Clarence always knew he would not marry anyone from his hometown. When he moved away to New York, he carried with him the history of his parents, even though he didn't understand it all. When he started to write poems and prose, however, he came closer. A Chevrolet, a pink and blue flowered satin dress, and slow dancing to the music on a hardwood floor above lake water, beneath the stars. A couple who fell in love and started a family in a small Midwestern town not far from Kentucky. A young man in search of his future, a half pint of whiskey or sloe gin in his sport coat pocket at Saturday night dances. He needed to get away, but after he left he discovered he could come back home by picking up the pen. The story of the girls and the boys in the band. A pink rose. History. Memory in the making. The story of a life, multiple lives of different generations, opening like petals in the pink rose his father once gave to his mother.

An Indianapolis Wedding

Dots and Clarence decided to elope, to avoid fuss, keep it simple, and avoid expense, so they drove north to Indianapolis and got married on February 13, 1943 in the side chapel of the new Cathedral of Saints Peter and Paul, at Meridian and Fourteenth. The bride and groom planned no reception, but his sister Verena and her husband, who lived in a small house on Livingston, in Speedway, near the racetrack, hosted a meal to celebrate. Older brother Edgar reserved the chapel in the cathedral. Clarence's parents, Benno and Mary, drove to Indianapolis for the wedding and the dinner. Bless us oh Lord and these thy gifts, and bless this couple and the children they dream of having. The newlyweds honeymooned downtown in the Riley Hotel that night and next morning drove to Louisville to visit her mother and sisters. Dorothy's oldest brother Alfred, who was married and now ran the family farm, became godfather to the couple's first son; Clarence's older sister, Flora, the godmother. The first child came into the world nine months and one day after the wedding, on a Sunday. According to legend, a Sunday child has special powers. To write, to look back, to foresee, to show the past as part of the present and the future, to show that all times and people are one? Times and things change, people move on, but this couple always came home to the place they loved. Historical novelist James Alexander Thom, a native of Owen County in the southern Indiana hill country, once said that home is where you want to be buried.

American Dream House

New neighbor Marcus Kuper built a sturdy brick house on a hill behind the new Holy Family School, on the edge of a woods still being logged. Cattle skulls and burnt stumps on the ground behind where the new dream rose and took on a roof. The American Dream for the working class: to have your own house in which to raise your family, but every dream is joined to its related nightmare. Clarence could not stop worrying how to pay off the new house, and there had been, two years before the move into the American Dream house, the birth and death, the dream and the nightmare, of the stillborn daughter, Marilyn. Dorothy would sob at pivotal moments in the dream house, such as when she and the three boys, Norbert, Edgar (named after his uncle), and Lenny, a baby wrapped in a blanket when they moved in, and Clarence knelt around a bed to pray the rosary. How hard is it to lose a daughter in birth and your husband must be sent to Our Lady of the Peace in Louisville for electro-shock treatment? The dream medications, which also created monster nightmares, were not yet developed. When Clarence was away, the modest but sturdy American Dream house was eerily quiet. Time, an abstract concept, stood still. This stillness magnified every sound, intensified every ray of light, every level of darkness descending. Marilyn must have been looking on, from another dream world, looking at the bedroom that would have been hers. But after Clarence rejoined his family, another girl, Mary Lou (middle name after his sister, Louise) was born. She stayed in this world, to grow up in the American Dream built on its underbelly nightmare. With the arrival of a baby girl, a daughter, a sister, the house was full. Dorothy started to hum and sing again as she did her work in the kitchen, where light entered more easily, and out in the garden and flower beds, where sunlight washed her face clean.

Dots at the Wheel Alone

She wanted to drive, to be more independent, so he tried to teach her how early in the marriage. No go. He could not rise above the anxieties still pressing down on him from a late-night crash after a Saturday night dance in another town. He shattered his kneecap before they started to date. Always, the pronounced limp. In the hospital, they gave him, unbelievably, the wrong kind of blood and almost lost him. Could not tolerate any uncertainty about anyone else's driving, the total lack of control that came with it and had caused the cruel late-night crash. She made one mistake that ended the lessons: hit the accelerator instead of the brakes and they shot through an intersection, narrowly missing another car; but when he died of a heart attack at seventy-five, she learned how to drive in her sixties and did not look back. Her world was not large, but now she could move around in it freely. She drove to the bank, the grocery store, to her brothers', sisters', and friends' houses—and out into her beloved country, to look at the hills, the woods, the fields, the barns, the farmhouses, like the one in which she had grown up. For some sixteen of the years she outlived her husband, she had good travels within the familiar world she knew and loved. But as she turned eighty came accidents, putting it in drive when she thought she was backing up to leave the bank, putting her foot down on the wrong pedal...

A Nightmare in the Belly

Then came the pain in her stomach, the weakness, the never feeling well, and the collapse. Her old faithful but now part-time doctor, who should have retired years before, misdiagnosed the problem as "a recurrence of diverticulitis." More time, which translates into life lived, was lost. The internist knew better: advanced lymphoma, the debilitating cycles of chemotherapy, the occasional decent day, a rare good one. "What did I do wrong?" she wanted to know. Before the chemo began, the oncologist inserted a needle into bone to draw a marrow sample into a syringe. Dots did not flinch, said proudly: "I'm still a country girl." She was tough. Well into the treatment, the oncologist announced, "It looks like she's going to have some quality time" and said she could stop the chemo. Within a month, the lymphoma was raging again, and she announced: "Enough, no more chemo, no more blood tests, no more needles, no more nothing!" She asked her granddaughter Elizabeth, a freshman in high school, to play the Schubert "Ave Maria" at her funeral mass. On Long Island, Elizabeth prepared the piece, rehearsed it with her New York City violin instructor, got it all right. She played with such feeling at Holy Family Church, Jasper, Indiana, across the street from Dots' house, that everyone marveled at the granddaughter's artful control. We gave Elizabeth's and Daniel's and Shane's and Erin's grandmother to the earth the farm girl loved, placed her next to the husband buried on the same hillside eighteen years before. We said our Auf Wiedersehen—not so much "goodbye" as, in the literal translation, "Until we see you again."

Dots' Legacy

Dot's four children could choose as many quilts and candle-wicked cushions as they wanted, from the beds in her American Dream house and the hall closets upstairs. Quilts she made, or had made, of plates, stars, squares, triangles, circles, and a log cabin in blues pinks, reds, greens, and tans. Cushions she candle-wicked, with stitched figures of bears and butterflies, pineapples and tulips, and angel wings, to give to a relative or friend who had a child or grandchild. The oldest son took boxes of family photos left over after the others chose, sepias of relatives and ancestors from both sides of the family, the unclaimed boxes when Dots' mother Mary died seventeen years before, of certificates, often in German, of baptisms, First Communions, and weddings, as well as school certificates and commendations, boxes of Krapf family materials left behind, as well as his own Little League and Boy Scouts and high school sports memorabilia stored in Dots' attic. All these boxes, repacked and reinforced, made their way to an attic on Long Island, but when the firstborn moved back to Indiana seven years later, to resettle in downtown Indianapolis, he brought the boxes back home. He gave them to the Dubois County Museum, formerly a plant of the Jasper/Kimball Corporation, in Jasper, Indiana, so that all the ancestors had an American Dream home in which to live for as long as time ticked on. Now ancestors on both sides of the family, as well as contemporaries of Dots and Clarence and their children, look down at people from within frames on the walls of the County Museum.

A German immigrant trunk that Dots gave to her eldest son and his wife and children, still full of American Dreams, with nightmares lining the bottom, stands in the immigration room. A glass-door bookcase facing the gift shop houses Dots' copies of her son's books, full of dreams and more than a few nightmares, stitched or glued and bound to last, signed, and inscribed to his mother. A bouquet of roses in memory of Dots.

V. Behind the Kafka Curtain

Bohemian Wine Glasses

My wife wants to buy Bohemian Crystal wine glasses at a bargain price in downtown Prague before we leave the ancient city. It is Saturday and the shops close early in the afternoon. She gets in line in the shop and I take the children outside and play games with them in the cobbled square, buy them ice cream, have them make drawings, walk around the block, make up jokes, sing songs, pretend we are characters in German fairy tales. We switch back and forth between English and German for two hours while their mother waits in the slowly diminishing line. She fantasizes about the dozen delicate, beautiful crystal wine glasses with flowers etched on their sides. Oh how gorgeous they will look in our house, she thinks, all dozen of them. She will pack them ever so carefully when our year in Germany comes to an end and carry them onto the plane and keep them in her possession to protect them. How exquisite these glasses will look when they catch the light from the chandelier above the dining room table. How good the Franconian wines will look and taste when we and our dinner guests sip them at table, Sylvaner, Müller-Thurgau, Riesling, Bacchus, Gewürztraminer. Oh elegance. Compliments from dinner guests. How much did these exquisite glasses cost? Oh no, that's impossible, not that cheap! But there are only six left when my wife finally reaches the front of the line. She takes them, crestfallen.

Approaching the West German Border

As we approach the German border, we pull over so that my wife, who does not like border crossings, can sit shotgun while I drive us into the customs zone. As soon as she gets seated to my right, she opens her purse and starts to panic. Her passport and the childrens' and their exit visas are gone, gone, gone. "Be calm," I tell her. "The children!" Later, she would remember hearing the sound of a zipper being unzipped. That would be the zipper of the side pocket of her purse in which she kept her and the children's U.S. passports and Czech exit visas. Didn't even see or feel the deft hand slip in the slide pocket and remove the official papers that were on the street and sold on the black market pronto. "Gypsies!" the Czech people would later say. "The Gypsies did it. Do it all the time." All for six wine glasses. And how many coins?

Children's Art at Customs

We try our best to remain calm. As we approach the crossing, two young Czech soldiers greet us in German. It is dusk. We have little Czech money left, little gas in the tank, and want to get back to West Germany and go to sleep. When I explain what happened, in German, the soldiers panic. They are on our side, say this is terrible. "It is not so bad for them," one of them says, pointing to the children sitting silently in the back seat, "but it will be horrible for you! We will have to call our boss." Meanwhile, the children are making colored drawings of the friendly young soldiers. They know the soldiers are on our side. They want them to be our friends, rescue us, open the gates and let us go home. People are people, they believe. They put all their charm, all their talent, all their hearts into their drawings. They believe their art can save our lives, make the gates open, and grant us permission to drive back to our apartment on the Other Side and fall asleep because we are good people, a nice family who want only to go back home and go to bed. God is on our side. Their drawings are beautiful, full of flowers and smiles and young soldiers with big beautiful hearts, but the gates are locked, the system is closed, and the sky is turning dark. The drawings do not work. The boss says we must turn around and wind our way back, up and down the hills and around curves, all the way back to Prague in the threatening night. We have to get new papers. Nowhere to stay, nowhere to put our heads down on pillows for the night. No open sesame. No magic spells. No fairy godmother. No charming prince. Only frogs croaking as we pass. All doors closed. All towns shut down on Saturday night. Very few lights in houses in the villages. A narrow road that is swallowed up by the dark. No full moon to light the way.

Phone Booth in a Czech Village

Little daylight left and we stop at the first public phone booth in the first village after being turned back at the Czech-German border. I dial the American Embassy in Prague, as the guidebook advises Americans to do in such an emergency. Connect with a young man who identifies himself as a U.S. Marine. I explain that three of the four of us had American passports and Czech exit visas stolen. I'll call you back in fifteen, he tells me, what's your number? Sir, I tell him, that's impossible. There isn't a phone number anywhere in this God-forsaken booth in this remote village near the border. Well then, he says, you call me back in fifteen. When I do, he says he has both good and bad news. Good: we can come to the American Embassy late the next morning, a Sunday, and they can have passports ready while we wait because we had registered ours at the Embassy in Bonn the previous fall. Bad news: It's going to take us at least four days to get new exit visas from the Czech government. They don't move very fast, he says. You'll have to find a place to stay tonight on your own. We can't help you. Good luck. See you tomorrow.

Nocturnal Tour of the Countryside

Good luck, yes, in the nondescript, shuttered dark. Good luck passing the old buildings so drab the notion of fresh paint applied to their walls seems absurd if not impossible. Good luck driving your kiddies back here in the oppressive silence. Good luck in finding a filling station open to fill up your almost empty tank on a dead Saturday night. Good luck in keeping your spirits up. Good luck in preventing your tired and frightened kiddies from having a panic attack. Good luck, Mama and Papa. Good luck, little brother and big sister. Good luck, Americans (two born in Colombia) stranded in a Communist country with no American passports, no exit visas, and no official identity or statehood. Only Papa, who has a passport, is legal, but his exit visa has expired, so he's legal only in the country where he was born. Goodnight Franz Kafka, German-Czech author of the nightmare visions. Pray for us now, Franz, in the hour of our need. Good night, boogie man. Good night, over and out in the Communist dark falling like dirt everywhere around and on top of us.

Biker Gang and Communist Police

In the fading light, we cruise down a long hill toward a village below. A truck ahead of me creeps along. No way we have time to poop along like this, I say to myself. We got to get to Prague. So I pull out into the narrow left lane and pass the truck. Veering toward the right lane, after passing, we hear a deafening roar come upon us. Five or six bikers in black leather jackets pass us while I'm still halfway in the left lane, as if sucking us up their hot exhaust pipes. When I'm almost altogether back in the right lane, a belated roar swoops down on us. A loud pop as another biker catches us and goes ahead. Gone, side mirror. Dangling, biker's arm. After we roll through the comatose village, we see the police out ahead on a level stretch of narrow road with the black-jacket bikers slouching at their side.

A cop waves me over, pointing to the broken wing of the last biker. Did you . . . ? Ja, I reply insistently. That will be 1,000 Kroner, he announces like a judge. Wait till you hear what happened to us, I blurt in my anxiety-ridden German. Before I can finish our story, he says, 500 Kroner! He stuffs my money in his pocket. God bless the Communist police. God bless the crippled biker and his rebellious friends. God bless our family. Are You there, in this remote and forlorn Czech countryside? If You are, please send me a signal. Give me some light from beyond. So many miles to go before we sleep, and where? I can barely see this road that snakes along in the dark.

Dancing Toward Prague

Call it a country dance, a slow Czech waltz. We inch through the black night toward Prague, stopping in every town and village where a phone booth is visible. I drop coins in the slot, dial the number of the man who rented us his old apartment on the outskirts of Prague. The phone rings in an apartment in the downtown that belonged to his late mother, but Milan is not in. We waltz from village to village, town to town, from the German border to the rim of Prague. I drop coins and let the phone ring, ring, ring. Never an answer. Nobody home. No place to stay. Nobody to talk to. Finally, the dull lunar glow of the ancient metropolis that fronts magnificent architectural examples of every style and period, but they are in such disrepair the sight makes you want to weep, if you can see it. Now I can't. Franz Kafka's ghost walks these streets, haunts these buildings, whispers lamentations in the ashen dark. Speak to me Franz, call me and my family home.

An Illegal Night in a Volvo Wagon

We park on the remote street beneath the high rise in which we stayed, a concrete building so drab and dreary it has no face. Every twenty minutes or so I walk to a phone booth around the corner to dial Milan's number. Please, a place for the children to sleep, a cushion for their heads. Ring, ring, ring. Everything is empty. Almost all the lights above our head go off, one by one. We are convinced that where light burns sits an agent of the state, spying on us, waiting to turn us in. He's reading Kafka stories about people trapped in their tortured existence, no way out, no explanation, sending in reports by phone: Yes, the children are still sleeping in the back seat. Yes, parents in the front. Yes, they have all four fallen asleep in the car. Yes, we can arrest them in the morning. All night long, as I drowse and wake, drowse and wake, my feet do a slow Czech waltz. I am waltzing into the center of Prague, but my partner is asleep in my arms. I am waltzing her along, on my feet, into town. Where are you now, Franz Kafka? Where do you wait? Would you do the Czech waltz with an American who speaks German? Who loves your stories? Tell us another one, Franz. Make one up, you German Jewish author with the dark imagination. Talk to me, Franz, in the hour of our need.

The Story of Franz and Max

Every day we are back in Prague, we must take the subway all the way across the city to the customs police office in a big gray concrete building. We must check on the status of our new exit visas. Without these papers, we can not leave the country. Without these papers, we are in the country illegally. Everything is beyond our control. Trapped, like characters in a Kafka story. Every day we take our subway ride to check on our identity, to see if they have given us one. Will they let us go? When? Why not now, why not, Daddy, why? Why don't they want us to go back to Germany? How long, how long will it take? Not far from where we get off the subway train lies the Jewish Cemetery, where Franz Kafka is buried. We find his tombstone and pay homage, before we visit the customs police. Not far away, we find the tomb of his friend Max Brod, his literary executor, the man who refused to honor Franz's decree to burn all his unpublished manuscripts, the tales and novels that have become classics. Thank you, Max, I say to myself. *Ganz herzlichen Dank!*

Greg's Weird Story

One day I tell the children a story as we walk up the subway steps to the Bureau of Customs Police and look up at the gray Czech sky. Once upon a time there was a man named Gregor. Guess what happened to him when he woke up! Tell us, Dad. Well, he felt really sluggish, even worse than usual. Just couldn't move in his bed. Why, Dad? He felt around his body and discovered it had changed. How, Daddy, how? Would you believe he'd turned into a humungous bug? Oh yuck! Yeah, he could just barely turn himself over in bed and flop onto the floor. You mean he was a big, sort of like a human cockroach? Oh how gross! Yeah, and he was late, late for his job, and that upset him. You see, he supported the whole family: his mom, his dad, his sister. That's not fair, Dad. Right, he was late for work, he didn't want to get fired, he was a good worker, but things were out of his control. Poor old Greg! Know what happened when they knocked on his door to tell him to put a move on 'cause he was late? What? Dad, tell us. That he had no voice. He could not talk. He had no human voice. He was trapped inside his bug shell. Couldn't get out, sort of like us trapped here in this country. Hey, Dad, my son says the next morning as we get off the subway and walk up the steps, tell us that story about Greg again. Tell us what happened to Greg. That was a good one. Really weird, strange. I liked it. Funny but sad. Kinda cool. Who wrote that story? Did you make it up? Tell it again, Dad!

A More or Less Happy Ending

One day after we walk up the subway steps and talk to the man at the desk who displays the photo of his children in a frame and is always kind to ours, we are given our exit visas. We return to our Volvo and drive back to the (West) German border. All the Czech people were kind to us. The lady with the holes between her teeth, in the Kneipe, the bar/joint next door to the drab apartment complex, she who gave us a bar of chocolate for our daughter. The woman in the grocery store who warned us not to buy those particular eggs because they were not good enough to cook and eat. The waiters in the restaurant who brought us our meals and a loud horn they squeezed, like characters in a comedy routine. Milan, "our landlord," who came over one night to drink beer and rail against the hated communists because they prevented him from going to law school, to get back at his father for operating a sand quarry and oppressing the workers. The beautiful young high school girl with "the Madonna forehead" a German colleague told me I would find. She carried a small spiral notebook, was interested that, as an American guest, I taught American poetry in Germany, and touched me by saying she enjoyed reading Walt Whitman's "I Hear America Singing." When later I stand before my seminar room in Erlangen, I find that the secretary has posted a note on the door to my students, written in a beautifully expressive passive voice: "Professor Krapf has been prevented from coming to class today." Jawohl! Unless prevented from doing so, I'll see you again somewhere, dear Franz Kafka, dreamer par excellence of universal nightmare tales

VI. Old Language, New World

New Language

In the Old Country, we chewed strong cheese, sausage, and black bread. Worked the fields of the Archbishop, and prayed to his God. Nothing was ours. First chance we got, we hit the Big Water and never looked back. Then we swam in the darkness of the wilderness. Nothing was the same. Not the trees, the birds, or the animals. And the new language tasted strange in our mouth, but those born here swallowed it better. Still goes down hard for us old ones.

Missing Old Earth

What and where is home when you know nobody or nothing and the terrain does not accept your footfall the same way, the seeds go in the ground differently, and the air enters and leaves your lungs like a foreign element? Who can eat freedom? What's heritage but being tied to the earth where you live? How can you be buried in a soil you do not know? Be rained on by water that comes down from a sky you don't recognize. Pray to a God who speaks a foreign language? Oh for a taste of the familiar and the sound of a tongue that sings a music that lifts you up and carries you beyond yourself.

The Sound of the Old Bells

We pray in a new church so small it would seem God barely fits into it. Rarely hear a priest say mass in a language that speaks to us. In the day we cut down trees and at night we dream we are back in forests we remember or rivers whose currents and bends we know. We recall the clang and pitch of the old church bells we left behind. People whose names are the same as ours we mostly left behind, but many of us have transplanted our language into the dark loam of the new soil. This earth we must learn. May our children bury us well.

Entreaty to Be Remembered

When we axe down one tree, another looms larger. Who could be equal to the shade that falls everywhere we step? When will sunlight be able to find where we stand and bless us for more than an instant? What hope brought us here? What prayers will fit in our mouth and find a way to plead our case for a better life? May our children and theirs remember this journey we took for them. Bless them with a strong sense of memory.

Those Left Behind

May those we left behind never forget us. May the graves we did not dig and the coffins we did not make for them be good to those we loved. May the rain fall gently upon the earth that covers them. May their spirits live forever above and beyond the earth they loved and be waiting to rejoin ours. May the spirits and the Spirit be with us for the rest of our journey and throughout our sojourn in this land that called us away from what we knew and loved. May we be called home again when the time is right.

New Prayer

May we learn the names of the trees and come to recognize the songs of the birds. May our seed take to this new earth. May our children be safe in a land that is strange to us. May the promises made to convince us to come here be kept and may we find new friends to help us put down roots and become part of the community we miss. May we grow enough crops and raise enough animals to eat on land that is ours to own and work. May our hands and backs be strong. Give us the strength to never give up and the faith to believe that our children will always be protected. May our children look up to us and remember us well. May our names endure on stones they have carved to stand above where we lie.

Legacy

A hundred years in one place and a home we can call ours. All the elders buried in good soil they called their own with stones that announce their names and dates and birth place and words from the Bible to commemorate their lives. Houses with good roofs, trees to give shade, and gardens in the back yards. A church near the center of town with a stone tower you can see from every street and alley. Bells that toll for every death. A sense of belonging and a need to preserve our story for those who follow. Give us a pen that will tell others who we were, why we came here, and how we worked together to make this good life. Let this pen show that a man or woman need not be famous to live well and be loved or do great deeds to be remembered. Show that a small life can be deeply lived leaving a legacy that sustains and nourishes.

Those Who Leave

Most stay but some will leave. Most of those that leave will come back to see those they love, but some may go away and never want to return, except for funerals and a wedding now and then. Some may not come back for anything. Some may have been hurt by someone or something that was here. Some may have known they could not be fulfilled by what they knew was here. They may have needed what they knew they could find only somewhere else. Some may have been driven to get away but then discovered it would be good to come back to what is familiar and eternal. And those who stayed and could not bear the thought of leaving will smile when their classmates move back to town but sigh when they hear the names of those who left and never came back. They might not remember that once upon a time some who lived in another country far away could not believe that some of theirs were leaving to go away and never come back.

Good Stories

Some will think that a story is interesting only if it happens where you do not live. If a story happens to you where you have always lived, it is not worth sharing with others. The assumption is that you have to go pretty far away to find a story that anyone will want to hear. How could a story that happened to little here be of interest or significance to anyone from a big there? Aren't the bigger stories about important people from big and fancy places? How could a worthwhile story ever happen to little old here? Wouldn't it take a really big imagination to tell a good story set here? Who's got the talent and vision to make a story like that fly and signify? Oh no, they say, it just won't work. Besides, we already know everything about here. What's left to learn? We need to get away from here to expand what we already know. Nothing important could come from here. Nope. No way.

About Here

Only reason he writes about here is because he left a long time ago. If he had stayed here, I bet he would not have written so much about this place. I mean, who couldn't become a writer if he moved to New York? Doesn't just about everybody who goes there become famous for something? It's easier to see things from there. So maybe if you went there you could write about here. Yeah, that's the only way it could work. You stay here and you're one dead writer. Not a famous dead male author, like the ones they always make you read in English class, but a dead author who never had anything to write about and died of writer's block because there is simply nothing here worth writing about. Amen. Oh sure, there's him, he may have left and come back and still has stuff to say, but that's because he was in New York so long. You live there long enough and you write or you die real fast. That could make you write about here. That would do it.

VII. The Minnesota Minstrel in Manahatta

Welcome to NYC

Welcome to NYC! This might not be the City of Love, but it was a good place for a guy from the small-town Midwest to make his name as a singer and songwriter in The Village. Came from out of nowhere, on the trail of the great Woody Guthrie. There's more than one poet made a name for himself here too. Walt Whitman loved to walk these kinetic streets and rode the omnibus up and down Broadway after crossing over on the Brooklyn Ferry. Absorbed the sounds and rhythms and songs of the street. Loved to drink beer and talk poetry and politics in Pfaff's in The Village. Manahatta, Manahatta, city of poets from all over the states and the world and singers of every manner of song from almost every kind of heart in every country! Who still hears the song of America singing? Who, in Walt's time, wrote mysteriously rich letters to the world that never wrote back? Even if she, Emily Dickinson, our other greatest poet, never lived here, her spirit too abides in the air. Here comes the boy from the Heartland, too, to sing his song and make his way into the world.

Highway 61

My name to some is Tambourine Man, Minnesota Minstrel to others, but I play keys as well as the troubadour's guitar. Some would say I ain't got no voice, but what kind of ear does that mean they have? Ain't they never heard the talkin' blues? Ain't they ever been out on Highway 61? Never been to the Delta? That old blues highway leads to the foot of this stage, and well beyond! That highway runs through all time and back into my gruff voice and will run long after I'm gone and my song continues to play. I'll take the twelve-bar blues any old day. I'll do my shuffle and have my say. If we write and sing well, with feeling and vision, our song outlives us all. Let us sing and tell our tales small and tall. Yeah, I got those old walkin', talkin' blues. Start up the bus, crank up the guitar, let's get out of town and go on the road again following that old vagabond Mr. Blues. Woke up this mornin', felt around for my shoes . . .

Texas Hothand

I usually bring along a Texas hothand, an ace guitar slinger. We were together for a time before. Once upon a time there was Robbie, now there is Charlie. And once, in that time of first electricity, there was Hothand Michael. It all comes from the Delta, the blues, and then to and from Chicago, South and West Sides, and it's always there to be connected with and carry us along forward, if that's where we want to go. Go back to the source, young man, go back, if you want to live the eternal life and be lifted up to something much larger than your Self. It's bigger than any one voice, any one vision. Go back, young man, go back to your roots to move out and on and ahead.

Sometimes a Whole Band

Sometimes a whole band makes the trip. Tony plays a strong upright bass and George pounds the drums real good and steady. Donny, smiling Donny, sitting or standing behind me, plays just about every instrument that fits a hand. Stu is over in the corner strummin' rhythm guitar, like a leftover folkie from the early 60s, or before. Like Woody? Who says this land ain't our land, as long as we stake our claim by the song we sing and how we serve it to the folk? Orpheus, Pied Piper, Tambourine Man, Troubadour, Minstrel Man, Minnesinger, Jongleur, Griot, Shaman, Bard of the American Dream and Demons Dark, people will follow if you get the lay of the land and the slant of the folk into your song, get it to flow like blood, and give it a beat like the pulse of the place where you were born or have come to feel at home. If we make the right turns, any direction can bring us home.

Busy Being Born

Some say I got too many styles, too many phases, too many voices and selves, too many identities and masks. They say I ain't nothin' but a homeless shape-shifter, a Gemini Janus who worships change. They say I ain't got no center! Some say that means I'm "fake." Can one person have too many traditions to draw on? Too many ancestors? Too many relatives? Too many homes in which to lay down his head? Too many stages from which to sing? Ain't nothin' to worry about, my friend. Got to keep movin' on, keep explorin', keep growin', keep pushin'. I ain't the kind who grows by standin' still. I got to move on, head out for another joint. As I once said, he who's not busy being born is busy dying. To be born means to keep movin' on. There was once upon a time a Mr. Jones who didn't get it. He's got lots of descendants too. But you and I, we get it. We been through all that. We know better. We got faith in rebirth. We know we shall be released. Born again in the waters of old-time song, that greatest of religions. Lift a tall one and chug it down for all eternity! Always and forever on the road with a song.

A Mouth Harp

Sometimes I speak through a mouth harp. When I do, it's as if shootin' stars rain down on me. Rainmaker, rainmaker, do your dance so the stars shoot down on us. Song and dance man, open your mouth and shuffle those feet. Give us your heart and give us your dark American dream. What else you got to lose? Give us some Midwestern soul. Shaman, shaman, heal us with your song! Somebody play that little man with the big song some tambourine! Let him dance free riding the midnight images and cascading rhythms of the song he hears from beyond. Follow him down to the water. Let the surf suck at his toes as he dances in the slipping and sliding sand just as the newborn sun rises out of the horizon to the East. Wave after wave breaks on the shore where he sings his amniotic song. Mr. Minstrel Man comes crawling out of the sea once again with foam bubbling from the lips that shape the sounds of his original song. Somewhere nearby sings the sad, high, and lonely song of the mocking bird, the musical shuttle, loser of his mate. And not too far away in the Paumanok swamp sings the sad and shy song of the hermit thrush. Ah, all American songs be one. Sing one for us, Minstrel Man, feisty little brother, sing us to new and eternal life. Make us forever young. Bring us together as one through the gift of your song.

Ringmaster, Center Stage

Here I go again on the harmonica. I like to play it center stage, as if I'm the ringmaster of my own show! Sometimes I can blow it all night long, yeah! Sometimes the harp is a voice, sometimes a percussion, sometimes a staccato backbeat, once in a while a melody, and sometimes a choir. Sometimes it speaks in blackface. It's amazing what can come through a small body and flame out charged with spirit from beyond! Blow and suck, blow and suck the spirit in and spit it back out! It ain't nobody's to keep. Share the American musical wealth, my friend. Something so big got to be passed on. From one clan and tribe to another. Share the wealth, give everybody a piece of your apocalyptic song. Brother Bard, Mr. Minstrel Musicianer, Songster, Bluesman, give us yet another demotic sacred song.

Just Because I'm Seventy

Well just because I'm over seventy don't mean I can't pluck some guitar! When I play a solo, buildings stand up behind me. What a feeling of omnipotence. They didn't have buildings like this in Hibbing, but we had some mines down the street. The man who can write a great song can make his own buildings, mine his own ore, hit the sun, moon, and stars, and then walk down into the basement for a bottle of Burgundy and move on to the harder stuff. The same is true of writing poems and songs. It all depends on how hard and long you want to go and when you want to wake up. Here comes Mr. Newly Awakened Man, Mr. Born Again Songster, ready to pass on through this little town. Come see his show before he hits the road again! Break open a bottle of his best garage-brewed song! Step up and get your medicine! Mr. Minstrel Man, he got all kinds and styles of musical medicine for anybody and everybody. Yes sir, yes ma'am, step right up! Save your body and save your soul! Take a sip of his ever-lovin', soul-savin' American song.

Roots, Man, Roots

That Donny can play a mess of instruments behind me, steel pedal, lap pedal, mandolin, banjo, violin, viola. I like it when he plays steel pedal because it reminds me of my country roots. Like a lot of poets, I'm always renewed when I return to my roots. Roots, man, roots, gimme roots. Gimme origins. Nothing opens up into the eternal now like the mystical moist night air pursuit of roots! Heritage, Hoosier or otherwise. Words, words, words. Sometimes when I get into the lyrics and realize they are poems, I forget about an instrument and just chant the words, words, words. Ride that bronco! Go with the rodeo! The white Stetson resting atop my graying curls helps me serve up words to the forever young at heart. Inside time, outside time, time out of mind, time out of place but in the right place all at the same time. One time, one place, for all people, inside and outside and beyond time. I sing for myself but I also sing for you, baby blue.

When I Play My Guitar

Sometimes when I play my guitar and sing, my shadow grows so long in the night I rise higher than the tallest building in Manhattan and I split the full moon in two! More light, more light, as a German poet once said on his deathbed! Poets, poets, they speak in my song! They are always a welcome foundation in the house I build with my song. Some would say I gave poetry back its old home in my ever-evolving song. My friends know that Allen G / sings with me! Call me Mr. Music and Poetry Man. Only a fool would deny it's best to live in the largest republic of heart and spirit we can create. I heard there was this Indiana Poet Laureate was in a "Hoosier Dylan" show that includes my buddy Johnny Prine's lead guitarist Jason Wilber. Well, I heard this guy has some poems about me in a book, *Songs in Sepia and Black and White*. I may read it one day or night, on the sly! I heard he lived around NYC for thirty-four years, overlapped some with me my second time 'round there, came to Gotham a youngster from the Midwest, like somebody I know! He even stole one of his poetry collection titles from a song of mine, *The Country I Come From* [is called the Midwest.]. Well, good thieves pay homage when they steal good lines, in poetry or song. Ain't nothin' better than a literary thief with good taste!

Norbert Krapf, a native of Jasper, a German-Catholic town in the southern Indiana hill country, taught for 34 years at the C.W. Post Campus of Long Island University. In 2004, he moved to Indianapolis with his family and served as Indiana Poet Laureate 2008-10. As IPL, he promoted collaborations and the reunion of poetry and song. Since moving back to Indiana, he has published a CD with jazz pianist and composer Monika Herzig of Indiana University, *Imagine—Indiana in Music and Words*, and has also collaborated with bluesman Gordon Bonham, with whom he worked in the Hoosier Dylan show. His recent work also includes a prose memoir, *The Ripest Moments: A Southern Indiana Childhood* (2008); *Bloodroot: Indiana Poems* (2008), 175 poems selected from those written 1971-2006; *Sweet Sister Moon* (2009), celebrations of women; and *Songs in Sepia and Black and White*, with photos by Richard Fields (2012). His most recently completed poetry manuscript, centering on childhood sexual abuse, is entitled *Catholic Boy Blues*. Winner of the Lucille Medwick Memorial Award from the Poetry Society of America, he was Fulbright Professor of American Poetry at the Universities of Freiburg (1980-81) and Erlangen-Nuremberg (1988-89) in Germany. He recently held a Creative Renewal Fellowship from the Arts Council of Indianapolis to combine poetry and music, with an emphasis on the blues.

More information is available at www.krapfpoetry.com.

www.ingramcontent.com/pod-product-compliance
Lightning Source LLC
Chambersburg PA
CBHW071231090426
42736CB00014B/3040